Coda

"Those masterful images because complete
Grew in pure mind, but out of what began?"

~ W.B. Yeats:
from, *The Circus Animals' Desertion*

Collections of Poetry in English

Blunderbuss (1971)

Apu's Initiation (1974)

Tomcat (1980)

The Hiroshima Clock (1990)

Coda (2022)

CODA

Selected Poems

a fifth collection of poetry

by

Rupendra Guha Majumdar

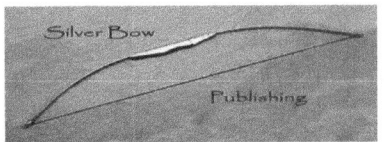

Silver Bow Publishing
720 Sixth Street, Unit #5
New Westminster, BC
CANADA V3L 3C5

Title: CODA
Author: Rupendra Guha Majumdar
Cover Art: Sculpture of Buddha & photo: Rupendra Guha Majumdar
Cover composition: Mrittunjoy Guha Majumdar
All interior Illustrations: Rupendra Guha Majumdar
Layout and Design: Candice James
Editor: Candice James

All rights reserved including the right to reproduce or translate this book or any portions thereof, in any form without the permission of the publisher. Except for the use of short passages for review purposes, no part of this book may be reproduced, in part or in whole, or transmitted in any form or by any means, electronically or mechanically, including photocopying, recording, or any information or storage retrieval system without prior permission in writing from the publisher or a licence from the Canadian Copyright Collective Agency (Access Copyright).

www.silverbowpublishing.com
info@silverbowpublishing.com
© Silver Bow Publishing 2022
isbn: 9781774031971 book
isbn: 9781774031988 e book

Library and Archives Canada Cataloguing in Publication

Title: Coda : selected poems / a fifth collection of poetry by Rupendra Guha Majumdar.
Names: Guha Majumdar, Rupendra, author.
Description: Poems.
Identifiers: Canadiana (print) 20220168520 | Canadiana (ebook) 20220172781 | ISBN 9781774031971
   (softcover) | ISBN 9781774031988 (EPUB)
Classification: LCC PR9499.3.G69 C63 2022 | DDC 823/.914—dc23

Bio Data

Dr. Rupendra Guha Majumdar is an academic, poet and artist. He has taught English and American literature in Delhi University and Suffolk University; he has been a Visiting Fulbright Fellow in the English Department at Yale University in 1981-82 and 1992-93 and Fulbright Scholar-in-Residence in Suffolk University, Boston in 2014-15. He has published four books of poetry in English from Writers Workshop, Calcutta: *Blunderbuss* (1971), *Apu's Initiation* (1975), *Tomcat* (1980), *The Hiroshima Clock* (1990). His poems have featured in anthologies in India and abroad: *Modern English Poetry in India* ,ed. P. Lal (WW,1971); *Indo-English Poetry in Bengal* (WW,1974);*The Oxford Book of Animal Poems* (London: Oxford UP, 1992) ; *Spotlight on Poetry: Poems around the World 3* (London: Harper Collins, 1999);*The Golden Treasury of Writers Workshop Poetry* (Calcutta,2009); he has translated Rabindranath Tagore's Bengali play, *Roktokorobi* (*Red Oleanders*) into English for *The Essential Tagore* (Harvard University Press & Vishwa Bharati Univ Press, 2011); his poem, "Searching for an e-Book in the Spring," was published in *Salamander*, No.41(Boston: Winter 2015),182-183; and his poem, "Pausing at Tao House" was published in *The Eugene O'Neill Review,* Vol.37, No.2(2016),271-272. *Coda* is his fifth collection of poetry in English over fifty years.

Coda

Coda

To

Karabi
and our sons
Mrittunjoy and Tirthankar

In the light
of the
only truth
that radiates
within

Coda

Coda

CONTENTS

1. Marriage and Prehistory, Endnotes / 11
2. Temple Street, New Haven / 12
3. Durga's Battle / 13
4. Beauty and the Beast, a Memory of Ghent / 16
5. World Cup Football: The Goal / 18
6. Second Baby, Age Two / 20
7. Coda / 21
8. Yale Baby / 22
9. 'Spithead,' Bermuda / 25
10. Kargil: Voices of War / 27
11. Riding Poorva Express / 30
12. Landscape of a Scholar's Table / 31
13. Bamian Buddha Blues / 32
14. Rawalpindi Cricket Test Match 2004 / 35
15. Sacrifice / 37
16. Surreal Sunset care of Salvador Dali / 39
17. Pompeii at Noon / 40
18. In Limbo, Coetzee's Michael K. / 42
19. Ashoka's Lion Capital, Kingly Quartet / 44
20. Boys will be Boys / 45
21. Metro Suicide / 47
22. Sunset Safari, Sariska Tiger Reserve / 48
23. Elegy to a Dove / 49
24. Revisiting Bruegel's *Landscape with the Fall of Icarus* / 50
25. Day of Judgment / 52
26. Achilles Heel / 53
27. Neeraj: Javelin Gold in Olympics '21 / 56
28. Nostos / 58
29. War of the Worlds Story / 60
30. Pausing at Tao House / 62
31. Searching for an eBook in the Spring / 64
32. Tribute to Ustaad Bismillah Khan / 66
33. Cinders / 67

34. David and Goliath, an Encounter / 68
35. Candles. / 70
36. Dolphins in the Time of Corona Lockdown / 72
37. Nocturne: Gautama Steps Out / 73
38. Ode to My Fiat Millecento 1100 /75
39. Grand Canyon, Notes and Queries / 77
40. A Haiku, to Life / 78

Coda

MARRIAGE AND PREHISTORY, ENDNOTES

Nascent anthropologist, she is primogeniture bound.;
Munia delves into artifacts of Time,
closely wraps, in blue cellophane,
a femur or ulna or petals of skull-bone
bearing coded sutures that could, Darwin-like,
damn lemur, marmoset or man in seconds.

The 'tools' of her trade are not metal made
with handles of honed antlers of antelope
but are potsherds and rocks of the tumescent earth:
useful pumice chisels once, rice-bowls,
duck-shaped ladles now freckled with silver lichen
in this brimstone-May when we novices of excavations

seek official marriage witnesses
who will absolve our union in retrospect,
sign and stamp on court-paper and form,
then assemble our fern-like fossil bones over millennia
and say, spectacles slipping down pachyderm noses,
'Ah! This is no Lepidoptera or Coelacanth pair

but hominoid upstanding Man and Wife
who lived happily ever before, buried
under the sandbanks of yonder Full-Moon river,
exiles surely, wanderers through pine forests
with lapsed passports,
                          lapsed countenances
    glinting
            with myriad stars
                      of silver-lichen.'

Coda

TEMPLE STREET, NEW HAVEN
Along Temple Street beside the central Green/park in New Haven, Connecticut, stand three churches in a row, built during the Puritan times of the first settlers in the 17th century.
*

All these years upright,
*three hou*ses of God
elbow to elbow on the Green,
is a bit too much,

since it was
pilgrims who were
supposed to converge there,
not walls of stone
turned eastwards
to give thanks for
small mercies rendered.

But watch!
At dusk, the three towers
become the blunted trident
of the bronzed sea-god*
poised for recompense
for all the children
who did not reach
this Green square of grass
       to feed
              the pigeons,

their small hands
still push the wracked   waves
onwards,
   their breaths lift the seagulls
gently
       over the foam.

---

*Bronzed sea-god : Poseidon, Greek god of the sea,
       sometimes realized as a bronze statue

Coda

Coda

DURGA'S BATTLE

In Indian mythology, Goddess Durga fights an epic battle over ten cosmic days with the demonic Mahish-Aashura (Bull-Titan) to restore peace in the universe, her ten 'arms' (daasa-bhuja) being symbolic of investments of power from varied divine sources in one complete warrior. The battle signifies a triumph that is celebrated annually in India — mainly in Bengal -- every October, to this day.

*

Far from losing heart in the throes of battle,
(sixth day running without a break),
he decides to don the rough autumnal hide,
hooves 'n' horns, tenacious muzzle,
accoutrements of the squint-eyed bull
so much larger than life blazing recalcitrant fire
and with more than one death to spare
      by divine sanction.

His carbon-dusk brow is one eddy of frowns.
Pressed contours on tide-splayed sands.
Being who he is, demon esquire,
he stamps prime forests, caravans,
pilgrim-staked precipices down avalanches,
playing his last pawn-shop protean card of grim disguise
to break, then drive the last keen-eyed,
kohl-eyed definitive goddess into the dust.

Later on, the "Bull" epithet would straddle his name:
they would say (in the mythic vein)-Look! There!
He who has demonstrated the bullish role,
      worn the bull-attire,
demon extraordinaire *Mahish-Aashura*,
master-bull, bull of many turns,
bull-devil of the Karakorum fen,
      who cares for none,
great gods, or men, or women,
nor up-market goddesses!

Coda

But then, alas! a crick in the neck proves fatal.
Pity, he cannot turn his head or shoulders in time
with a flick (as big bulls do if gnats bother)
when her true lance descends
with a sharp rippling twinge of rending
deep in-the flesh of the collarbone
into his black surfeited heart
from the most unexpected angle --

for which she, in looking larger and higher,
standing poised aloft the tawny feline back,
fiery-eyed, breathing hard,
                   has surely her charger,
the lion-king, to thank.
          He whose claws ripped open
              the end-disguise,
                       held down
      the bull's tumescent breast
              beneath
                         her foot.

Coda

BEAUTY AND THE BEAST, A MEMORY OF GHENT

1

The setting's in Ghent—fairytale Castle Gravensteen,
Le Chateau des Comtes—a mile from the station
framed by canals, cobbled streets
and shadows of oak forests
that stood gnarled and twisted in the wind's sway
                once upon a time.

Now sleek-nosed trams hum
and swing out of brownstone corners to a halt—
a flash of yellow, white, and blue
press on twin tracks of steel — then quickly disappear
past the edges of tall glass mugs of beer in roadside pubs,
beaded froth of tourists spilling across ivied flanks
                of this medieval city.

The walls of the castle (which I finally enter)
are of lichened granite soaring skyward with the wail
of damned inmates whose thigh bones splinter apart
as the spokes of the wheels turn slowly to their screams
of "Mercy! God mercy!" and the efficacious mid-afternoon
                cracking of rib after rib.

Room by room I walk guided by white painted arrows;
neatly displayed and captioned are hatchets and pikes,
a pitchfork to hold up the newly chopped head,
screws for thumbs in various shapes and sizes
of peasant or squire who disobey the call,
and the deadweights wrought in iron
to stretch the kneecaps or hip-bones from joints
                till the ligaments snap in meandering cries.

2

In his own castle the Beast abounds
growling over his spoils, no doubt a magical place,
a garden of golden corpses under a blistering sky

Coda

as the sun comes down past the casements,
then the blue moonlight couched in cobwebs
lurks in the wake of swallows.
Storm clouds burst and splinter to
                          with a lie.

On her, the distraught damsel, is bestowed the role:
To stake her millennium beauty and soul,
make it binding with a kiss unprompted,
alone for a tryst with the Beast *within*
                          waiting for succor.

Will she do it? Can the marriage of opposites,
beauty and beast, lord and serf redeem?

3

My brief itinerary does not furnish the answer.
I start for the railway-station in one more yellow tram
quite uncertain about the lessons of the past hour
and peering into a future equally unclassified,
no museum tag attached to the legacy acquired
        through plan or chance.

The gates of Gravensteen loom large behind me
as I walk briskly away, turning only once
        to look over my shoulder at a sound
        which seems, I reckon,
                like running
                      footfalls
                              in the summer wind.

Coda

WORLD CUP FOOTBALL: THE GOAL

A reigning monarch of the Ball,
say Marcelo Salas, Baggio or Batistutam,
pursues it like one possessed
on a stream of coloured motion
       (of myriad hues)
that twists and turns
over the liquid grass
and hurtles to the goal.

       An acute angle drive—
       after superb piloting
       through the cutting reefs
       of boots and brawn, swings
       into the Defender's ken
       as he takes the anger
       of the Ball upon his chest
       in a rainbow of startled sweat.

A virtuoso tackle, a second's
impasse: the tide withdraws
and turns to the other end
with rapid strides ushered
by the seagull cries of the referee
(of the nimble toes) who can afford
to take no sides when either strikes —
though only he can attest the sovereignty
of the blow.

       In the minutes passing,
       muted explosions ruffle
       the air as the Ball dances
       across wind-blown fountains
       from side to side, boot to boot,
       in great arcs of shots
       or straight ground passes
       that race the blood's
       sedentary trot, the clock's
       intransigent shuffle.

Coda

Then, well into the second half,
one explosion sounds louder still,
marking the crescendo of a *GOAL!*
The crowd announces it in one
cumulonimbus voice,
the referee too with biting whistle.
The killer Ball is through
and beyond the invisible wall,
on its axis spinning
like a dam-busting bomb
till ensconced, winded in the net.

        Quite the high-water mark
        of a summer song—a *GOAL!*
        No author could be prouder
        of the outcome of his inward strife.
        Whoever's done it has done the needful —
        Maldini, Ronaldo, Suker, Diego
        or Alessandro, Del Piero or Platini —
        in the last breath of the game's life
        when all the chips are down
        and the time's up.

As sudden and drastic
Is Death's own thrust in broad
daylight or midnight squall,
        we mortals fear.
Woe to the hapless loser on land
or sea when the Ball is through,
between the bars.
The winner takes all
      for a while—
           and there's many
a hand and tongue
           to cheer.

Coda

SECOND BABY AT AGE TWO

He likes the feel
of fountainpens
in his new world
fingers.

His eyes reconnoiter
the horizon of pages
as his bits of doodling
stumble

and slide over
each other like
waves over shiny
boulders

in the foothills
of the Himalayan
mountains.

His monologues are
often inconclusive
in thematic content —
but what of that!

His kind of words
possess the projected
élan of the frontier man
unmindful of the final

      call of worlds
           closing in
  on

      themselves.

CODA

The wind takes care
of the dust on chairs.

The doors of the forest
are shut on strangers.

I await the noon rush
of tribulations,

the pressing of feet
on golden sands.

Coda

YALE BABY

      In March 1993 the city of New Haven faced a massive snowfall which brought life to a standstill. For my wife and I, living in the city, the impasse was very worrisome as we were expecting the birth of our first child any hour; and most roads leading to Yale New Haven Hospital were snowbound, cabs were out of circulation. Then things took a new turn.

*

1

He bypasses his "due date" in March,
forecast by Dr. Reeves. Fourteenth.
No great hurry, still verrry cold outside
and snowing. Most blanche New England
winter in a decade radio 'n' all concurred.

Surely, far better within the cove
of Majoni's womb than riding high,
bronco-buster, all strapped up
in the car-seat of the Chevy
though that nice girl from Tennessee
promptly here may be at the wheel.

2

Black sonogram dots of eyes
stare back at me unblinking, large forehead,
pear-shaped cheeks, hard midfield soccer
kick on muscle wall: all prove he's more
than embryo, less than precocious puck
        for all seasons.

Limbs precisely folded
like an astral parachutist's,
he procrastinates on the threshold
of lapsed salvations
before plunging head-first into the abyss
of our sleepless nights with a howl.

Coda

We bide our time, nestle into # 816, State
and Pearl, large cubish red brick corner house,
"oldest on the block", two miles from
the 20 York Street Yale Hospital helipad
of his dinner-time landing.

3

Eighteenth. Above the seafront the sky darkens,
sways and stumbles, splits down its sides
with a grimace, spine a bow-strung
wracked vertebrae of lightning; winds spew
a whipcord of a blizzard down avenues
of the worn Ivy-wreathed Connecticut brow
        of the Atlantic.

"Storm of the Century!" repeats Channel Eight
with dread as Elm and Maple branches,
knocking on our windowpanes freeze.
Parked cars snuggle into the snow like huskies
        after a run.

4

Twenty second. A blue unblemished sky
all clear and sparkling. Seagulls saunter
like grey haired bankers on the Green.
Regular checkup for mom-to-be at eleven.
We catch the 'Q' downtown bus to the Yale Rep,
then walk three blocks.
                Past the swivel doors,
                      inside
    we await our turn.

Through the monitor screen, darkly again,
the stare. Unblinking, poised within
a close umbilical twirl, he reckons it's time.
Outside, temporal sirens unfurl their tongues.
We dash home in Lydia's timely car

Coda

    to return within the hour
        and clinch
the tidal spasm of pain that birth prescribes.

At quarter past nine, with red lips pouting
through memories of galactic sleep, he meets us
on our grounds without more elaborate stance
  or press comment.

      We apologize deeply
           for the stiff itinerary.

    Surgeons gone,
        left alone, we bow
           to a destiny
                of loving.

Coda

SPITHEAD, BERMUDA, 1999*
 Eugene O'Neill's erstwhile, shorefront-villa, 'Spithead' in Bermuda in the Twenties, was the venue for an international conference on the playwright in January 1999; which I happened to attend
*

I will write as I please — poised precisely
for a while on a middle path —
about any igneous thing on earth:
a fringe of mountains in the Hindu Kush
or a lost continent biding time,
or that sequestered fish-hook island
in the upper reaches of the North Atlantic
I reached last winter in a rush.

Laced with lichen of many hues upon
a scaffolding of coral, the place preserves its secret
in dolphin guarded coves of lucent crystal I've only heard about
but never seen or slept within during nights
of Nietzschean tempests when sky and ocean
break even their millennium fast with a ritual sacrifice.

In the glistening harbor of my room's mirror,
a white cruiser floats anchored in the middle, motionless,
a lone seagull after a squall, resting its feathers.
Our first day abroad bears the loss of an hour.
We adjust our watches over breakfast following
an uninterrupted shower: we behave like familiar natives

of the place, white skin or black or in-between, not
unduly shaken by 'recorded' mysteries of warplanes
that once just disappeared into the black holes
of radars across the horizon of strife, we put on
the straight academic face, no staggered wrinkles
on the brow like the countenance of the lagoon
in downtown Hamilton, calm, untrammeled as if
           by seismic tremors.

Coda

The writer who lived here once (no, not me)
also stood before the mast in weathered dungarees —
from the Caribees to Buenos Aires,
flicked his black hair across his brow,
his eyes carried the swell of the ongoing surf
in a backlash of tears for sons abandoned,
        misbegotten, wandering in pain.

'Spithead', his mansion at land's end lapped by waves,
looks like a ship with its sails down and folded in the locker
while moored in a lush equatorial cove,
no hands on deck, awaiting sealed orders
(when all are back — captain, first mate and rotgut company)
to start the throttle under a darkening sky

for an undisclosed passage, a voyage
of primal reckoning
        when the dead awaken
              and the curlew sings
        at the edge
              of the broken shore.

---

*Published in *Laconics*, eOneill.com, Vol. 6(2011)

Coda

KARGIL, VOICES OF WAR
The three-month long Kargil War of 1999 saw Pakistan and India at loggerheads in the North-Western frontier, it being the fourth incendiary confrontation since Partition in 1947 over the Kashmir issue.

*

     Still
    spinning clockwise, inclined
twenty four degrees to the right, our Earth
plays up its given centrifugal role,
hurtles forward on its own axis-heel day and night
     around the sun,
        spitting out
            the indigestible seeds
   of bullets on either side
            of the cosmic track.

Still, shell-shocked, the summer air traduced
the stringent act of breathing in hewed pulses.
Infants, mothers, mothers-to-be whimper
in the throes of wrested sleep, in makeshift houses
far from their own — scraps of rotten pinewood,
tin-sheets and tarpaulin held upright
and then lashed together with twine,
anchored against the windblown fury of God and Man —
     deep in the ransomed valleys
  of Mashokh and Poonch, Kargil and Dras.

These hills have borne witness to ages
of scavenging: birds, beasts, avalanches of savage
horsemen have spewed from the volcano's mouth
brandishing *Timur-naamas** of death when cities have
laid down to rest, ignorant in sleep, inured to pain
when the entire world slept soundlessly, when
no time was left for laughter or furious commands
barked out at dusk with filial voices
and the thud of drums dislodging the dew
on blood-red Oleanders and Flame-of-the-Forest.

Coda

Are those wolves lurking in the shadows eyeing
morsels of humanity on platters of gold?
Now above the mountain stream's commotion,
before the break of day, shells twist and scream
        a diatribe of death.
Deserted, lie the border villages, walls, and roofs askew.
They echo the night-long barking of dogs
that have all perished on a landscape
                of pained surprise.

Who are you, pale warriors with unkempt beards,
prompted into battle with no cause of your own,
pupils dilated and shifting
        like beetles on storm-tossed branches?
What madman has pushed you here — bulls prodded
across ripe fields of corn to claim these meadows
that many covet though none can grasp
or finally possess
        or ever in this life really shall?

Tololing is back in our hands, Batalik too.
Daily we throw the dice with the cock's crowing
and the bugle's call; we have our briefs
committed to memory in the instance of capture —
our brains will not bear downloading!
Just think. In the chilled, disjointed trajectory of the wind,
the souls of our dead and tortured pilots have surely undone
            the Stinger's** bite.

Daybreak tomorrow shall measure the last assault
up the hill of the Tiger. The stakes are few
and far between and clear at a cutting price
that we each, if summoned, shall pay just once.
To recapture what is ours — nothing is lost.
We have some hours left to lay down our cards
as the flames flicker like wild ravenous birds.

Coda

Are you ready to charge
                        in the name of progeny living —
    and of those in the womb as yet
                              unborn?

The snow, the rolling breath of epic mountains,
descends on every side, impervious benediction
on fallen sons lying in obeisance between the boulders
with arms outstretched above their heads,
faces down upon the breast of Earth Mother —

                All listening to the pressing boom
of a great heart's beat across ravine and sky
            and distant ocean.

Beloved,
        will the flakes of white
            forever bury
                the flagrant red
            that blood deploys in spasms
                    from the broken sinews
                              of the soil?

    **Timur-naama*: echo of the *Babur-naama*, the 16th century memoirs of Moghul Emperor Babur who was a scion of his ancestor, Emperor Timur
    ** Stinger missile: heat guided air-missile.

Coda

RIDING POORVA EXPRESS
Remembering Mother

*

Mother's awful state
recalls me to her side.
I do the thousand-odd
eastbound miles in
a rounded dusk and day
riding pell-mell Express Poorva,
wheels clashing
through the May night's
brimming tunnel.

Hoping she's still smiling
there above the black loam
of our town's crust,
sitting upright on her
ruffled bed as I enter
with furrowed brow,
a beating heart.
A silent intruder
expecting
        the worst.

Hoping she's still there
to receive me warmly
as I turn the courtyard corner
by the well, to clasp me
to her chest, her youngest,
dearest son...
        to hear the thousand
thudding echoes
    of those wheels finally
merging
        into One.

Coda

LANDSCAPE OF A SCHOLAR'S TABLE
To the memory of Sisir Kumar Das (1936-2003), eminent litterateur, poet, playwright, humanist, Tagore Professor in Delhi University

*

We recall, at certain moments
of the summer day, memories
through a clouded sky:

in the landscape
of your substantial table
viewed from high
stands a clutch of pens
and pencils like icebound, moulting
tree trunks biding for spring,

a few terraced mounds
of darkening books harvested
under a rally of storms; and one
peerless, windblown mountain-peak
on the table's horizon—

    -- you!
with a balding pate, poised
comfortably in your chair, musing
over a succeeding generation
of peaks along a never-ending range
    east and west,

womb of mighty rivers (in Almora) once
witness of the parturient *bhairavi**
songs of sunrise
    a son sang softly
to 'Maharshi',** his father.
    The inundating brook—your mind—
searching for long-lost dulcet voices
in the woods, still flows
    through our bereaved valley.

---

*Bhairavi: a morning classical Hindusthani raaga; **'Maharshi': sobriquet for poet Rabindranath Tagore's noble father, Debendranath Tagore;

Coda

BAMIAN BUDDHA BLUES
    In March 2001 the world witnessed the destruction--by the Taliban sect--of the two colossal, fifteen hundred years old Gandhara statues of the Buddha in Bamian, Afghanistan, as idol worship was apparently anathema there.

*

To break a Buddha or two–
is on the agenda of these
mountain-goats with curly beards
          and killjoy eyes.

It takes them time
but they kick and they butt
with black hooves and horns
and keep bleating in unison
till dusk at his presumptuous
sermonizing in the middle
of the desert though by proxy
through loaded signifiers
of crafted stone, sand-blown
whispers of *Dhammapada* verses.

And that, while towering
a few meters just too-o-o tall
over their narrow shoulders
like a bloody colossus,
as a Roman consul called Cassius
had once said deeply scowling
about the upward mobility
of his king of kings.

And by God!
Dropping those millennial sermons
left and right like names
at dinner-table conversations,
sermons that have no business
to be there at all as statements
or minutes or in any shape, or form

Coda

to add to the protracted silence
of the desert air and to smother,
        haltingly, the echoes

of bazooka and other incendiary shells
that gnaw into the night, break into
the bodies of saint or sage or prince
or just your smirking roadside yokel
with no major stakes at all in kingdoms
of any kind, subject to the claims
of death, disease and age beyond
the brief lessons that time will teach.

They kick and butt with metallic hooves,
rudely blunted and cracked,
their horns askew triggering sparks.
"Goats will be goats" is the apocryphal cry,
for the dust to settle they give
        no time.

They grunt with the pain of disbelief,
the hatred of natural wholeness in
their hearts, their anger hammering
against the wide-eyed witnessing rock-face
of Bamian as it crumbles into wisps
of rasping wind over the mottled earth.

The hammering that persists
like the heartbeats of the damned
at the appointed hour
till nothing palpable is left
of the Tathagatha's* visage
and uplifted palm blessing
the wilderness of hearts with
not the least of mortal conditions.

His eyes, forever lowered, turn
further inwards poised over
the silk-route, the crossroads
of pain and human forgiveness.

Coda

Against a cliff of ancient
memory, north-by-northwest,
tall and very still,
           a shadow
                       of a shadow
   smiles
           in the moonlight.

---

*Tatha-gata: Buddha uses this name when referring to himself in the Pali canon; It means, 'the one who is beyond all passages in time and space.'

Coda

RAWALPINDI CRICKET TEST MATCH 2004
India's Cricket Captain Shaurav Ganguly won the toss and chose to field, as Captain Inzimam-ul-Haq of Pakistan looked on. India won the Test Series, 2-1.

In the third and Final (Rawalpindi) round
      of the Indi-Pak bash
we are miffed about the opening pair
in the batting line, the two
            who are to face
the walloping wind swings
of Shoab Akhtar and Sami without flinching
or detriment to our own vantage
on day One, Wednesday fourteenth.
Phew! Who has the clout?

In Multan *da mitti** and hoary Lahore
the story line was different:
we won the first, lost the second,
both clinched with thumping margins
that raised the blushes on the bristliest
      cheeks,

flummoxed the smartest willow-
scribes writing columns east or west
of the LOC for the extremes
of *Win and Loss*, chastisement
and praise of the two teams in so
      short a breathing time.

Consider this! Sourav's unexpected
return following his tumble 'n' toss
and Kolkata restitution, unwittingly
entails the axe for Akash or Yuvi
for the opening slot with -
master craftsman Sehwag.

But out of the blue, surprising all,
the darkest horse turns out to be
our school boy keeper, young Patel,

Coda

who for the benefit of skeptical eyes
lets loose like Chatrapati Shivaji**
Maharaj with his Castilian sword,

slashing the ball disdainfully to every
corner of the alien field in a fitting reply
before he is caught behind for sixty-nine,
his highest score as Dravid (the Wall)
takes over, with that glint in his eyes,
to make up for past lapses and Waterloos.
His 270 comes pat.

For us, the wind-gods have been quite indulgent
on this trip, our sailing's been fine.
Ganguly has expressed no need to bite nail or lip
or to fling off his shirt to make statements
of his inner tension below or above
                          the regular line.

He has been cool, even intently grinning
(when Shoab hit the six). So has Wright.
Not to beat Balaji and Irfan in the display
of gleaming dentition above the angle
of yanked, cart-wheeling wickets. And
           don't forget Tendulkar

who has capsized untimely. Twice!
So what! In the last over he claims
the last word against the Pakistani side
with a googly which Danish Kaneria wants
           to send to the Hoogly***
like an indigenously launched rocket
but which our dear captain catches with
a leap, a bounce, a roar—and the Series
is placed neatly
                 in our pocket!

---

*Multan da Mitti: the soil of Multan
** Chatrapati Shivaji: formidable 17th century Maratha King and warrior
*** Hoogly: the Hoogly River at Kolkata, arm of the Ganges

Coda

SACRIFICE
**On seeing the prehistoric skeletal remains of a
young girl in a museum exhibit, allegedly a ritual sacrifice.**

*

Under the eye of the full
moon they hold you firmly, limb
by limb, rough fingers on your
jaws down upon the black
granite block for sacrifices.

Do you recall the nubile
Iphigenia faced with midday lies
by the wind-dead shores of Aulis
on the verge of her 'propitious'
marriage to bridegroom Death?

In warrior guise, Atreidae* knife
poised at her throat; murky plot it
was, the queen mother said; now
you, your end today occurs on
the flat peak of the man-made

hill you are taken, head bowed,
to the top, a hundred rain-washed
steps on all four sides,
narrow drain down the centre for
spilt black blood to flow down

and congeal in indiscreet gasps
in a pool below, mite auspicious
for bathing the day after the kill,
till the gods are content with what
portions of faith you are bound

to offer; you do hear muffled
drumbeats clash 'n' call, of brass
cymbals, bugles, libation bearers
keening in fake despair; you see

Coda

the clouds above scramble
like Piranhas when man or beast
falls unduly into their current,
their confluence of teeth to forfeit
taut skin and muscle, nerve,
protesting soul in a matter
                        of seconds.

You see the moon above the hill
stripped of its ochre-parchment
skin; you see strips of moon-skin,
moon-bone, phlegmatic moon-blood
turn into vapour, into clouds

to journey to kinder planets as
the ivory knife curves deep into your
gullet to please the god, gild his
hyena grimace with your glance,
the touch of your breath.

You, fawn-eyed shepherd girl on
the last hillside, blue beaded bangles
on your wrists, head turned to
the east of your narrow shoulders to
kindle myriad sky-lamps
                    with your ebbing glance.

You are the white foam
                        of the cascading river.
You are the torn rose-petals
                    across the twilight sky.
You are the face
                of the approaching storm,
      the golden eagle's
                  homeward cry.

---

*Atridae: progeny of King Atreus of Mycenae, namely Agamemnon and Menelaus. Iphigenia was the daughter of King Agamemnon and Clytemnestra, whom her father was divinely induced to sacrifice for raising favourable winds to sail from Aulis to Troy to fulfill the Trojan War.

Coda

SURREAL SUNSET CARE OF SALVADOR DALI

The tree bows down to the winter
sun descending into the earth.
The cloud bursts into a paroxysm
of birds, Dali's travesty of Mirth.

The river twirls like a bloody
whip upon the flanks of twilight.
The tiger growls from a moonlit cliff,
warning presumptuous *Night*.

Coda

POMPEII AT NOON
Afternoon of August 24, 79 AD: Mount Vesuvius (240 km south of Rome) erupts spewing black fumes, ash, pumice and lava for two full days, silencing forever the unwary denizens of Pompeii.
*

From beyond the city walls,
Mount Vesuvius spouts its
foul madrigal of ashes upon
them all with
      a low peremptory growl.;
In the absence of shadows
at noon, there are no other
sounds besides the humming
unfamiliar tune descending
      from above.

The children on the patio
are taken by surprise by
the pouncing monster of
granny's tales, their homework
incomplete, school bell ringing
around the curb, their petrified
laughter saved for the itinerary
of two million tourists per year.
Pater's admonishing finger points
upwards at the renegade clouds
      of stifling smoke.

The public baths are brimming
with souls of mottled grey
mannequins twisted and still,
with no more berths left on
Charon's* boat to be wafted
across River Styx's black waters.
Salt waves wash the tracks of gods
limping hastily from the scene
of the crime beyond all reach.
A millennial quartet of dolphins
leap high into the air above the Bay

Coda

of Naples on the Tyrrhenian sea
framed within deep blue and white

mosaic walls, barking together all
at once like sheepdogs in search of
truant flock on a hillside scalded of
its skin of grass, soft footfalls taken
in surprise
        by an onrush
                of stealthy fire.

_____

*Charon: the ferryman in Greek mythology, who carries, in
his boat, newly dead souls across the River Styx to
the Underworld in Hades.

Coda

IN LIMBO, COETZEE'S MICHAEL K
for J. M. Coetze's novel, *The Life and Times of Michael K.*

*

Stopped
        in the middle of
the tarmac past noon ... duty bound
pushing his dying-mother-filled cart
beyond the city walls to the final
resting place she wants   her valley
of flowers

        he does
not speak out at once, his mind,
to the cops at the gate. They bark
at him in unison, their black pupil-less
eyes of guns turn upon his ribs,
stare past each blunted bead
of breath in alveoli ventricle or valve

        he knows
nothing moves till far into
the steaming haze
                not yet
the cavalcade of tall cacti turned
to the east, the field-rat or lizard
in acacia clad
            nor the lone vulture
high up above   in limbo
      nailed to
                the crimson sky

Coda

Coda

ASHOKA'S LION CAPITAL, KINGLY QUARTET
The lion-capital emblem of Emperor Ashoka (268-232 BC) — a sandstone sculpture of four male lions standing back to back -- signifying the Sakya (meaning 'lion') clan to which 'Shakyamuni' Buddha belonged, also projected Ashoka's commitment to Buddhism, following the bloody Kalinga War he had proudly led.

*

First you confront (in the image) just three lions
standing tall, shoulder to shoulder at ninety degrees
to each other, finely polished pink sandstone so that
only one pair of eyes unblinking meets yours straight on;
the other pairs, with steady eyelashes, couldn't
                    care less.

Two more profiles, mouths agog on either side, look
askance to East and West past the broken columns
of Persepolis in complete disarray not far from
the mud of Indus banks around the moon's
bejeweled ears — O hear! Now approaching close are
pounding hooves of a spectral black horse, Bucephalus,
                Alexander's shadow once.

But then, the fourth invisible visage in this leonine
quartet of pink rock-stars, being quite eclipsed
and turned to the rear, can hardly be checked
by noon, hidden from view like the dark side of
the moon we never get to see in print or cinematic
screen, no concave mirror poised above
                    to reflect its wounds and scars
                            in the desert's extended glow.

How poised, how frozen his whiskers are (Cat's
Whiskers, they call him still!), how primed for more
bloody wars with a lightning crackle in grim Kalinga,
bowed prisoners in tow, sinews drawing taut, reins
a-jingle the chariot of the sky's last Sun
                          — we'll never know!

Coda

BOYS WILL BE BOYS
"Militant attack on Pakistani school kills 132 children."
(Los Angeles Times, December 18, 2014)

As a matter of fact, the last
lesson of the term was
                      very brief,
and to the point,
               peremptory,
pressed by a penal colony afar to
scribble on their skins with
the blunted nibs of hard-nosed
bullets in rapid succession.

They lay down one by one
obeying a curfew of "Sleeping Time!"
on the surface of the earth's
scarred womb, curling to their sides
knees bent, most fitting position
for extended slumber
          through storms forecast.

Now you can never say with that
tilt of your pepper and white head
of hair and piquant smile
"Boys will be boys!" for all
          grammar's grounded
into dust, the regular inundating verb
'to be' shunted into the past.

The tenses have turned rogue in
their fragile moorings, the future is
gutted into seedless memory in
the tense called *'future discontinuous'*!
All future that was. Here grammar
          will not work.
     Yet sentences are passed.

Coda

Boys will no more be
                    boys again.
Boys will no longer be. They were
called by the name of *'boys'* once,
gender checked at birth and noted
in the severed umbilical scribble
       of a midwife's diary;

only their names will presume
to be, become, to bind, disclose, break
even in the autumnal shadows of faces
and eyes, ready smiles dissolving
in a monochrome dusk —

Salim, Maqbool, Sayeed Raza, Ali,
Imtiaz, Shah Rukh, Nawaz — names
        windblown,
              floating unclaimed
like shredded
                untethered kites
     from the mind
              of a clear
                      winter sky.

Coda

METRO SUICIDE

Very thin
line between
body and   soul

take those
furious wheels
on a railway
        track the
woman's neck

placed on hold
for just a blinding
second in the
        glint of
the camera's eye

is enough to
            prove it

SUNSET SAFARI, SARISKA TIGER RESERVE

And they followed
                the same dusty track
dappled with footfalls — of a barefoot village girl,
herds of deer, peacocks, and the Sun —

     safari Land-Rover wheels
curving through the scrub, past watering-
holes, ravines,
        to the very edge of a memory of wars
                of a long-disputed land —

where twilight initiates its last murmurings
of bats, screech of owl, in-house crickets and
startled rabbits on the run one after the other
        past the thorny perimeters
                of a chthonic tiger's growl.

Coda

ELEGY TO A DOVE

I have seen at break
of day torn feathers on
the floors of houses,
bereft of body or beak
that in the midnight past,
poised on rafters, was
a whole much
       contented bird.

I did see at break of
day torn feathers on
the floors of houses bereft
of body, or beak, or eye
by mercy of quick
fang and claw of
spotted lynx, dispensed
of soul
       and song.

I may see as yet, waves
before the eventide
rebound against the cliffs'
white brow with the roar
of grace to scatter afar
her ashes now
       on borrowed
              wings

Coda

**REVISITING BRUEGEL'S *LANDSCAPE*
*WITH THE FALL OF ICARUS***

Daedelus, the divine artisan of the Labyrinth in Crete and the father of Icarus -- both being trapped on the island -- planned their escape by devising wings of feathers and wax; but tragically, the injudicious son *en route* drowns in the sea. However, Pieter Bruegel has painted this mythic scene, tongue in cheek, with a sardonic touch.

*

So many of these
moods or miracles
acts of saviours
just vanish from
your history's torn

undisguised pages,
witness to masquerades
of guilt slow frills
of silence

and holocaust dark
till crows recall them
insistent again and
again with

crackling voices as they
fly across the face of
a surf sprayed sun
thankful for life

for their still unburnt
feathers on wings
that lift them whole
into the purple air

only as high as
the altitude briefed
precisely by Daedelus
Labyrinth's spry master-
builder in Knossos

Coda

who rose buoyantly
into nimbus clouds
but did not fall headlong
in a swirling tizzy

like his precocious
wing-shorn son
wax undone Icarus
plunging into Bruegel's
uncharted sea.

Coda

DAY OF JUDGMENT,
MOHAN SINGHPLACE, CONNAUGHT CIRCUS, NEW DELHI

Forenoon of September nine —
a capitulation unforeseen; my two boys
touching eight and thirteen witness
a fall, a spouting of occult blood
                they may well remember.

Carried, on a stretcher, I join
the concourse of debility and pain,
my eyes are open wide, I see
the ceilings of meandering corridors
ripple and stretch over my head
towards an estuary of Intensive Care.
Glass panels gleam on every side.

Bottled salines suckle my veins
at needlepoint as they meekly shudder
and smart, turn sore, a bluish green
labyrinth merging into the distant
promontory of my knuckles
                at the outpost of my heart.

Oesophagus confesses erosions,
duodenum too, staring into the tiny
camera eye that delves into the lunar
lesioned landscape of my guts,
searching on and on for a more than
bacterial cause to pronounce
                        I ought to live or die
Or, briefly in between,
                merely pause.

ACHILLES' HEEL
**An epilogue to the Trojan War beyond Homer's *Iliad*
(which concludes with the death and cremation of Hector)
viewing the mortal end of Achilles, King of the Myrmidons.**

Listen, my boy,
for epic wars,
like this one
in Troy, the silent
message is clear —

you need to dig
your heels in
before those others
do as penultimate
act of fear and then
kill, kill, kill!

But that's hardly
ruse enough to
thwart Achilles from
glory while he
squares all accounts

of old in wild
Myrmidon eyes, fights
furious River Xanthus
to the teeth; next
drags behind his

chariot wheels, cold
Hector by his
heels thrice around
Priam's granite walls
before having his

Coda

own unanointed
heel undone by
just a long drawn
borrowed quick-
silver arrow

an afterthought
of a pretty lad
reared in the wake
of Troy's despair
and Helen's lust.

Coda

Coda

NEERAJ: JAVELIN GOLD IN OLYMPICS'21
Neeraj Chopra was the first Indian athlete to ever win the gold for javelin in the Olympics, held in Tokyo in 2021.

*

1

In bronze, head to toe
strapping fit Lord Poseidon
of the salt-waves with wash-
board abdominal muscles,
feet nimbly placed
wide apart, muscular left
arm extends horizontal to
his shoulder, poised
      straight forward

to balance the thrust of
the right which stretches
back raised in line with
the high crown of the head
to hurl his trident across
the Aegean — it fiercely
      whistles by.

Within the museum, he grips
no lengthy spear today —
it's long flown out of his grasp
though his right-hand fingers
are still tightly clenched like
an eagle's claws still clasping
the scruff of its ghostly prey.

2

Cut to Tokyo'21: "Action!" Last
pulse of the year's Olympics —
its "eternal" flame transported
from the hearth of Jovian
Olympia by a relay of feisty runners
bearing the torch to the far east,
land of the large red floating dot

Coda

of the rising sun.

It's the day after the anniversary,
seven decades past, morning of
the descent of the berserk atoms
of payload "Little Boy" * dropped
from bomber Enola Grey in '45 when
astral blossoms of mushroom clouds
rose high to bolster the reeling orange
confetti sky in Hiroshima, mon ami!

3

Neeraj of the tousled locks, just twenty-
three, Indian *fauji beta*** all set to flick
his ace, become a brand, begins his run
down the strip of synthetic grass
swings hard his yellow quivering javelin,
draws first blood, YESSS! a 'gold'
           in sports' Neverland —

quickly draws his muscles' reins not to cross
the finishing line with transgressive toes
as his right fingers let go — he brakes his pace
by rolling his body in a twisting dive
like a dolphin arching the twilight
                  surf to redeem
      a not so ancient
        forgotten
                curse.

---

* *"Little Boy" was the name given to the atom bomb which was dropped over Hiroshima, Japan from the U.S., B-29 bomber 'Enola Grey' on June 6,1945 as the final means to stop World War II.*
** *Fauji beta: soldier boy. The young athlete is a Junior Commissioned Officer in the army.*

Coda

NOSTOS*

They never thought I was awake
with eyelids half closed
deep within my mossy chamber,
                They never thought.

They thought I was still asleep.
They thought, smirking, I was gone afar
into the forbidden valley from where
few return by dusk up the swelling river;
but that there could be survivors too,
                They never thought.

They believed I was missing. Lost. Dead.
Whatever. And there was no forwarding
address. Nothing in bold Gothic font or italics.
They were sure of my cryptic undoing.

It was the peak of summer. Streets were
deserted. A cat meowed, ears flattened,
hungry as ever. I did not wish to swing
the millennium bell to break the silence
of my passage, my delayed return
that would make up for lost time,
                They never thought.

Maybe, at some point, I overslept.
Which does not mean I must shut eyes forever.
This sleep was in the cards, it could not
be dislodged. It could not ... not be.

It spoke to me, my sleep. It said, do not open
your eyes, do not open the eyes untimely,
do not pry open your inmost eye, pupil dilating till
your mouth can speak the Word in full measure.

I hear the wind in the avalanche
recovering its breath in spasms, lungs heaving,
memory-bowed, heart distraught but true.

Coda

The Word and the crumpled pages
of sleep go hand in hand,
wait for the final run,
                They never thought.

See! My lips can pronounce the Word.
My mouth slowly turns the Word with the tongue,
like a small, round, rare and bitter fruit.

I could do this. I could speak and bite, pause
        and spit, work sails to the wind
despite every Siren song, still live to tell my tale,
                      They never thought.

———————————

*Nostos: Homecoming (Greek)

Coda

WAR OF THE WORLDS STORY
Science fiction interlude for our times

1

In the War of the Worlds
chronicled by H.G. Wells esquire,
aliens trod the planet in armour

of colossi tall as giant Redwood
trees, fed on sinew and blood
of mortal kindred young and old

regurgitated into filigrees of
calcified pink lace-like epidermis,
lava cascading recklessly across

the landscape in acid snow-
flakes through the seasons,
burial entire of the colour green

by undulating folds of crimson.
Reign of Terror persists for more
than a year without respite -- sons

and lovers thrown asunder,
the odds being truly one sided,
man, from start to finish what

can any Tom Dick or Harry do?
Artillery fails to make a single
dent by bullet bazooka or bomb!

2

The piquant question arose:
what would these unwelcome octopi in
oversized armour consume for food

Coda

once cattle, human flesh and blood
ceased supply, rotting by springtime in
their guts when bloodletting turns soon

to the nightmare of ghosts of a long
abandoned earth left with no choices
but to chew each other under the blue light
                of the moon.

3

Then one clear day the giants are all undone,
notes the chronicler of woes, not by blazing
canon fire of artillery tanks but in a rakish

David-Goliath syndrome encounter: a rare,
bacterial assault on the collective cerebella
of the interstellar gang as overwhelmingly final
as a sledgehammer swung on one's
                extended toes!

A storm cloud of circling crows on high
announces the definitive global answer aloud,
flashing their beaks in the sunlight
      like black scimitars
           beyond
                  an unholy war.

Coda

PAUSING AT TAO HOUSE*
To the Memory of Eugene O'Neill: when he lived on his estate, Tao House, in Danville, San Ramon Valley, California during World War II; and where he wrote his best plays.

*

Long, long after the Gold
Rush he came out West
to California to garner
those nuggets missed by
the mules and the grizzled lot.

The shadows of Mt. Diablo
pressed athwart his rooms in
the house with the red-tiled
roofs called Tao across
the valley and the streams,

paused there amongst the narrow
bookshelves on the walls for seven
years before the mast in Melville's,
Dana's, Conrad's care past faint
cries of continents at war

and much besides to reach
the darkening roots of sycamore
and oak forged in lightning,
gripping the loose black earth
through his crowded dreams.

At the foot of the hill beyond
the barn, the gravestone of a dog
contains fond memories of a white
firmament of coal-black stars — Blemie,
constellation of the Spotted Hound,

Coda

Dalmatian soul poised unleashed
to walk the full distance
        of faith uphill
            as it listens
to a piano playing on its own accord
        the song
            of the distant
                moonlit surf

when all is past
        rebuke
            and so very
                still.

---

*Published in the *Eugene O'Neill Review*, Vol.37, No.2 (2016), 271-272

Coda

SEARCHING FOR AN E-BOOK IN THE SPRING *

1

I open Project Gutenberg dot com, place
the name of one Girish Karnad in the precarious
window above left of page and wait for available dope for plays
online, namely *Tughlaq*, for my English class in the spring term
come January *anno domini* twenty and one five,
we are counting the days.

Gireesh? Did you mean 'girl-fish'asks venerable Guten, curious,
bemused; 'garish?' or 'gish' or G(rendel) 'Irish'?, he queries,
a Tiresias groping downstairs. How could I reply?
How Girl-fish? Girl one end, fish-tail on the other, as Prufork
surmised to dare about the sweet mermaids singing each
to each while his bald patch shone like the August moon in
the middle of his sand blown hair.

Next — 'karma', 'karna',' kanard'? Perhaps 'konrad' with a 'k'?
like 'kyklops', the apple of Poseidon's eye, praying for recompense?
What would you prefer? His head upon a dish? Is it a heart
of darkness you refer? Are you now King Minos
musing over a June solstice, with your pet minotaur drooling
for a midday snack in your bone-laced labyrinth?

Take your pick — girl-fish, bull-man, centaur,
golden fleeced goat-boy with flute on Arcadian meadow or even
the Siren girl-birds in our deep blue Aegean who can sing
every homebound ship into black splinters on the rocks
with their lullabies of eternal sleep.

2

Do you have that in *your* memory, I ask Guten the Borg,
all that took place in happenstance in the not so familiar Deccan turf?
Are you alive to the deed, to the task? And can I have the substance
of my e-book back and my girl-fish too?
The silence is as loud as the crashing surf.
Birds were dinosaurs once

Coda

With footprints on the run, emblazoned
in rock, a stream of printed arrowheads seeking a heart.

And here's a strange, landlocked bird-form
a bespectacled seer found on Galapagos, named it
Ebok, after its call, as it walked on water, past grimacing eddies,

on the run, point of dim extinction, nay, extinct, a fate
of feathers undone,
                      mutely calling
unto the last, "Ebok, ebok!"

———————————————————

*Published in *Salamander*, #41, (Dec 2015), 182-183

Coda

TRIBUTE TO USTAD BISMILLAH KHAN
The great *shehnai* maestro Bismillah Khan of Varanasi expressed his deeply eclectic lyricism of Hindusthani classical music on the banks of the river Ganges where he lived and died.

*

Dawn sees the rose-tinted river
curving gently into the city
of ancient learning,
whispering
through his *shehnai* lips a *Bhairavi* pulse
of pure ecstasy
and pain unfathomable.

He bows to the river, his mother,
his father, his *taalim*.
Childlike, he grins
a toothless smile, then mutters in *riaaz*
a *thumri*, a *kheyaal*, a *Brajabaashi** song,
taps his bony fingers on his knees.

Elsewhere a known *Brajabaashi* couple
listens intently among the trees,
dances compulsively along!

By sunset he sits on the steps
of Manikarnikar Ghat, sips his regular
khullar measure of cardamom tea,
then plays to God and Man alike
his plaintive notes of reed music

that will bear his soul
to the horizon's edge
at the bend of the river,
       like a Bird of Paradise
               breaking free.

**Brajabashi:* denizens of Braj–Lord Krishna's domain in Vrindaban; *Bhairavi:* a morning classical raaga; *khullar:* terracotta cup; *taalim:* classical heritage; *thumri/kheyal:* genres of classical Hindustani music; ghat: public riverfront steps leading down to the water.

Coda

CINDERS

Sure, true beauty is there —
Whether it be in First Folio
or flower or in cascades
of rainbowed waterfall.

But what will I blindly sing
of the beauty spent, beauty
where it should starkly be
In unanointed king or queen?

On the *Gulmohar* tree
a resplendent bird is flapping
its mortal feathers to be
free while forests burn

to cinders the limping bird of the heart,
the golden cage, my mother's ribs,
which I can count one
by one before I turn the page.

Coda

DAVID AND GOLIATH: THE ENCOUNTER
"Let no one lose heart on account of this Philistine."
(David, Samuel: 32)

*
1

I will fight you, he cried
                and picked up a stone.
I will fight you, he said
                as he peered into those eyes.
I will fight you he thought
                touching the tousled
desert wind
        of his hair.
    .

Closing in on the stretch of no-man's-land,
girded with giant cacti on slopes and sharp cries
of circling kestrels, big and small meet
                at the level of ground zero

before a bolt of sharp lightning-licked sling-stone
cracks the wrinkled firmament
                of a behemoth's brow
    right
        at the epicenter.

2

Goliath sinks heavily in a cloud of dust biting
his own tongue of untested fear, his eyes roll
in the thick blood of his sockets, the champion
More-than-Man crashes in heavy armour
clanging to the earth, an overshadowing, gross,
over-the-top Philistine chokes on the ignominy
        of brute fangled words.

The immediate lowliness of earth serves
the pressing purpose of the unlettered,

Coda

unseasoned lad calling a spade a spade
                      knowing that customized
armour or helmet only pulls a big, blunted body down,
does not protect in battle — oversized shield, ornate studded
wrath of a gilded grimacing Medusa-visage of
                                no real worth.

The scimitar loosened from the big man's grasp
serves Dave's immediate purpose
                    of a neat *coup de grace* to
separate head from neck at the crucial turn of the spine,
a fountain spouts, congeals into the rarest of desert flowers.

3

Your young boy-shepherd counting his sheep
before the sun sets in the ravines -- he does
the honours, patriarch-to-be of the clan, no big deal, once
chastising stray lions or their snarling shadows
                        in the tall elephant-grass.

But here he raises high the disjointed trophy by the hair
against fleeting parturient clouds dripping a trail
              of purple blossoms.

Blood is real, thick, and glistening,
    this fountain of darkening blood
                          spouting for ages.

CANDLES

From
      darkness
to light is just
the angle
        of what
you perceive
        as true.

The uplifted golden
leaves of fire
      on tips
of candle-plants
concede as they
bend and shiver

      with the wind.
      A new
world in sight
that will not cease
to be
    when light in the west

sinks
      in my father's
        river.

Coda

Coda

DOLPHINS IN THE TIME OF CORONA LOCKDOWN

We heard shimmering grey dolphins
                were sighted in the River Ganga
at Hooghly, the water being easier
                to breathe in and out now
during Corona lockdown, they have risen
                from skewed graves to post
unsolicited messages of their own.
                                  Let them be.

Next are these ultramarine mosaic
                dolphins leaping over the wall
in Pompeii which got pressed and veiled in time,
                an unfolding curtain of volcanic ash
descending suddenly upon
                a mob of bewildered faces;

they carry messages, too, in brick, dust and lime.

                                  Let them be.

Coda

NOCTURNE: THE BUDDHA STEPS OUT

> If a man conquer in battle a thousand times a thousand men,
> and if another conquer himself, he is the greater of conquerors.
> – Gautama Buddha: *The Dhammapada*

1

Eyelids in downcast mode
                decisive as in battle
the man at the helm of things warrior still
acutely sure of the way the world's time passes

unshod you step into the night   in a trice
you give up the seen
       for the unseen
              the moon-struck future
for the now.

No one knows of your spring passage,
your breath of fragrant air. Only the dusk crickets
warble staccato tremors deep within your
extended plan, closely parley and pause knowing
full well a new war is in the cards while the kingdom
sleeps indifferent to the loud chronicles
              of frogs.

Beyond the walls stretch fields of corn.
River Anoma flows into the valley; blue jackals on
their beat nudge the full moon with moist
snouts, howl in unison at myths
             of shadows.

2

Your feet barely touch the marbled
outreach of the courtyard you quickly cross
to gain the final gate of the citadel you
know too well;
              moonlit aglow

Coda

the watchtowers, halls, endless corridors,
stepwells echoing footsteps, furtive voices,
the wind-stirred tinkling chandeliers jostle
as you pass recumbent shapes of guards.
You pass grey shut-eye pigeons nodding on
their feet
        for once untouched, unwrenched in sleep
         by the spotted lynx on his late-night prowl.

Ivory white your steed, Kanthaka, caparisoned for
this end, paws the soil by the gate, snorts acquiescence,
bears you quickly to the edge of the forest
from where
        one of your kind, forfeiting birth,
                never returns.

3

It's late in the gloaming, the moon's quite full;
your dream-eagle soars above the crescendo
of waterfall spray and wind in the gorge as pebbles
fly from under the hooves of your
            galloping war-horse,
       your head
   held high,
  crowned only by
        a hovering aureole
                of fireflies.

Coda

ODE TO MY FIAT MILLECENTO 1100

1

So difficult it is to pass judgment on an old car's worth —
after many moons of use and misuse on crowded roads
of the capital and on the Grand Trunk Road envisioned by
Mauryans and later, Sher Shah, the Badshahi Sarak* many
centuries old I have driven on from Delhi to Kolkata,
and once, pushing the four-wheel barrow a mile past midnight,
      on an empty tank while street-dogs barked.

She came here first from the east, a thousand miles along
the Gangetic Plains, taking a piggy-back ride in a rail wagon,
boarding at steel-town Durgapur, tethered with ropes to the floor
as they do in transport-ships ferrying cars and containers across
oceans,-astute vehicle, a gift, shipped across by father with concern.

It's complexion, black, auto pedigree noted in the Bluebook: Fiat
Millecento 1100, 4-cylinder carburetor engine chrome lined
flanks of sedan class with front doors opening outward like wings
of an eagle seizing the air over a fleeting rabbit which dives timely
into its air-raid-shelter burrow under a large Tamarind tree.

2

I board a bus for the Old Delhi Station yard to receive her --
she's laced in silvery cross-country dust, ensconced in darkness
among a range of household goods — two teak-wood beds, Godrej
steel tables 'n' chairs, almirahs, ceiling fans, utensils galore — all
appointed to set up a bachelor's Spartan flat and more.

A Murphy radio too with shining knobs; and one green mailbox
for receiving letters that mother wanted to write to me but
could not in the days given to her when the muscles of her deft
fingers stiffened much before the twilight when her time was up;

when her fingers, trembling unduly like her breath, could no longer
grip an ink-pen or spoon, or lightly touch the lineaments of her son's
face, its lingering scars, a face like mine, truant
                      and slowly fading

Coda

like a meteorite drawn into the orbits
of rogue planets of the galaxy.

3

Such an empty and expectant mailbox, transported
from far, resting earnestly in limbo on the back seat
        of the car, complete with latch, lock, and key,
                painted a light viridian green
on the back seat of the car (as the train hurtles on);

        foreknowing her familial shores, familial times,
        as it was, as it should be, a low murmur
        of four invisible cylinders in a protracted breath,
           my black Millecento
of multiple years, now unfettered and ready to go,
            moves on to better climes,
              no time for tears.

---

*Badshahi Sarak: 'Royal Highway'; the G.T. Road is 1500 miles long,
    stretching from Kabul to Kolkata; over two millennia old, from the times
    of Emperor Chandragupta Maurya.

Coda

GRAND CANYON, NOTES AND QUERIES

    On the brink of
your primeval canyon
the zany wind-sculptor of
these cliffs twists and
turns
    the lone pine tree
(deeply scratched all over)
into knots of passion.

    It pauses,
as you in white cotton
shirt over khaki cargos
and smile,
    hair streaming
walk
    into the picture frame.

It holds its breath as you
look into its blood-shot eyes,
sway drunkenly high above
    yon Colorado river

and ask —
    'Hey!
    Besides carving
millennial rocks with teeth
and claw and quaintly
    scaffolding
a buzzard sky -- what else
    can you do?

A HAIKU, TO LIFE

The wind, a sly sudden shark.

The leaves, small scattering fish.